This book is dedicated to Kendyl, Kade, Jordan, & Deborah Kozich for her amazing support.

My name is Grace. I'm eight years old and this is a story about my dog, Jobi.

Jobi is a chocolate brown labrador retriever... but what makes him special is that he can talk. You heard me right—he can talk. Last year we went to Hawai'i and brought home a magical collar, and our lives have never been the same!

Sometimes I wonder if Jobi really needs the collar to talk. Maybe he could always talk. Anyway, one thing is for sure. Jobi is the wisest, smartest person—I mean dog—there is.

I'm not an only child. My sister Faith is twelve years old and our brother Steven is five.

Faith and I love to shop... and shop, and shop, and shop. We love buying new clothes and shoes! Steven doesn't like to go shopping. He plays video games instead.

Anyway, that's besides the point! I'm trying to tell you a story about Jobi and Faith. She's pretty cool, but things changed when she turned twelve.

She doesn't want to play with me and Steven much anymore, and she really doesn't want to hang out with mom and dad.

One day last spring, Jobi and I were playing in the front yard. I was climbing trees and Jobi was laying in the sun. "Gee, Jobi, aren't you getting hot out here?" I asked.

"No, Grace, I rather like this time of day. It's such a quiet, peaceful time. I can just let my imagination wander..."

"I wish Faith would come outside. It feels like she's too busy for us. Remember how we all used to build forts and play games together? I really miss my sister, Jobi."

"Don't worry, Grace," Jobi said softly. "Faith cares about many things: school, her friends, and playing soccer—but she still loves you. Don't worry. One day she will realize that love is the most important thing, and she won't forget about her family anymore."

"Do you really think so, Jobi?" I wasn't so sure.

"Yes, of course. As we grow up, we eventually realize that living with love is what matters most. When we start giving love in everything we do, our lives become amazing!"

"Ummm… I think I understand you, Jobi… but isn't Faith just doing what she wants, like everybody else?"

"She will learn, Grace. And you and Steven will learn that love is the most important thing in the world. Dogs already know that! When you have love, there is no more fear. Not many people know this, but love can bring you courage and joy. You should try to live in love, Grace—loving our families makes our lives meaningful." Then Jobi laid down and went back to sleep.

Nothing much happened the next few days... until Mom and Dad told us they had some sad news. Our Grandma Sally had to move to a nursing home.

"What's a nursing home?" asked Steven.

"It's a place for older people who can't take care of themselves anymore," Mom told us. "Grace, can you please go get your sister? We're going to visit Grandma in her new home."

"No problem, Mom!" I yelled. "Faith! Steven! Come on, we're going to visit Grandma... we have to go NOW!"

Then I turned to Jobi and whispered in his ear, "You come too. I bet Grandma wants to see you just as much as us."

14

I didn't know if dogs were allowed in nursing homes, but I did know that Jobi wouldn't bother anybody. Faith, Steven and me all followed Mom and Dad into the car. Did they even notice Jobi getting in with us? Well, I sure wasn't going to point it out.

I kept wondering, How come Grandma had to go to a nursing home? Was she really sick? Jobi told me that Grandma needed help walking and eating and getting tucked into bed.

We drove for a very long time. It felt like we would be driving forever, and then finally we arrived. Whew! It looked like a normal building to me, but it definitely wasn't Grandma's house. The sign said: Whittier Nursing Home.

As soon as we walked inside, Steven started crying. "I don't like it in here! This place is scary," he sniffled.

"I know. Just look for Grandma. Then you'll feel better." Steven reached over to hold my hand. Meanwhile, Dad was talking to a lady at the big desk. He asked what room Grandma Sally was in, and if dogs were allowed. No pets allowed, the lady told him. What was Jobi going to do?

We all followed Dad down the hall to Room 125. Grandma was sleeping inside. She didn't look very good.

As soon as Faith saw Grandma, she wanted to leave too. "Let's get out of here... I don't like places like this!"

But Mom said, "We're not leaving yet. We're here because we love Grandma."

"I know Grandma misses us," I replied.

And then somehow, Jobi appeared! I have no idea where he came from. It was like magic. He licked Grandma's face, then she smiled and opened up her eyes. "Oh hello, Jobi!" she said. "How nice to see all of you!"

Steven kept sniffling, but Jobi sat quietly right next to Grandma. Everyone was petting him when a nurse came in and told us it was dinner time.

"But it's only 4:30!" I was so confused.

"Yes, Grace," my Dad said. "They like to eat early because the people who live here go to bed sooner than we do."

"It's okay, I'm starving," Steven said.

Dad smiled. "All right then. Let's take Grandma to the cafeteria and eat!"

I thought Faith was going to have a fit. "I love Grandma, but I don't want to have dinner with a bunch of random old people!" she whined.

Jobi had a twinkle in his eye. He looked at me and whispered, "I think something magical might happen here today."

"Sure, Jobi," I muttered. But I didn't really believe him.

Nursing home dinner reminded me of our school cafeteria, except it was super quiet, all the people were very old, and no one was smiling. It was like nobody was having any fun at all...

While I was eating my green beans and mashed potatoes, I heard Dad ask Faith to get up and sing for the old people. Faith ignored Dad.

"Please, Faith?" Dad asked.

"I don't feel like singing. I don't want to and I won't do it. Why don't you sing a song for them?"

"Your Dad's right, Faith," my Mom said. "You have a beautiful voice, and you could make everybody's day by singing one little song. It would mean so much to Grandma." Faith crossed her arms and turned away from the table.

Mom and Dad looked so disappointed. "Okay, honey, if that's the way you feel," they said.

Jobi popped out from under the table. We still have no idea how he got there.

He barked one time to get Faith's attention and then whispered something into her ear. She touched the coin on Jobi's magic collar, and suddenly had a huge smile on her face.

I guess everyone heard Jobi bark, because just then some guys in blue uniforms came running towards us, yelling that there are no dogs allowed in here. "Where is that mutt?" they shouted.

Steven cried and screamed at the top of his lungs, "Mommy!!! Mommy!!! Those men are scaring me! They're gonna hurt Jobi!!!"

And then Jobi disappeared in a flash of light. The guys in blue uniforms stopped at our table, but our dog was nowhere to be seen. They were so confused.

Steven stopped crying and whispered in my ear, "Grace, where did Jobi go?" Faith was looking around at all the people.

After the men in blue uniforms left, Faith got up and slowly walked away. I thought she was going to the restroom, but then I realized she was walking toward a little stage in the front of the cafeteria! All of a sudden, the light in the room got very bright.

I couldn't believe it when Faith actually started to sing. At first she was so quiet that we couldn't hear anything. But slowly, she got louder until she was belting out the song with a giant, sparkling smile...

Faith was like an angel with a golden halo of light around her. She sang her song without music, but it didn't really matter.

Everyone in the cafeteria was turning their head to see where the music was coming from. We could all hear Faith now—her voice sounded so sweet that it filled everyone up with love.

People all around were smiling like they had just seen a triple rainbow. The grandmas and grandpas almost looked like they were young again—some of them even had tears of joy in their eyes.

Faith kept singing in her halo of light, and it almost looked like she was floating above the ground... I was so happy I wanted to scream out. I know I'm only eight, but what I felt was special. Did I feel love?

Finally Faith sang the last words of the song and stepped down off the stage. There was silence, and then a few seconds later every single person in the cafeteria was cheering and clapping.

People stood up from wheelchairs and waved their arms. I'm sorry if this offends anyone, but everyone was acting like a child!

Faith walked back to our table and everyone thanked her on the way. Then things came back to normal.

Grandma Sally, who was crying, stood up to give Faith a hug. "Thank you Faith," she said. "Thank you from all my heart. I love you. You don't know how much your song meant to all of us!"

Faith was crying too when she said, "I love you too, Grandma."

On the other side of the cafeteria, I saw Jobi behind the food counter. He winked at me, then disappeared again...

After dinner, we left so Grandma could go to bed. When we got home, Mom and Dad gave Faith so many hugs and kisses. They kept saying thank you for her act of kindness.

Faith told Mom and Dad she loved them, and she even thanked them for being great parents! I still couldn't believe how different Faith was acting!

All that was good, but I still have to say this: The best part of the whole day was when Faith kissed Steven and me and tucked us into bed. She read us a bedtime story and told us she loved us... and we knew she meant it.

Just before I fell asleep, Jobi jumped up on my bed and licked my hand. I had to ask, "Jobi, what did you say to Faith before she sang?"

This is what he said: "If we love someone, we should show it. I told her that magical things can happen when we show our love. That's all—she did the rest. Grace, we all have love in our hearts. Magical things can happen when we realize that love is the most important thing."

"Goodnight, Jobi," I whispered. And as I drifted off to sleep, I wondered... Did Jobi make this happen, or was it just Love?

About the Author

David Kozich is an attorney, professional life and business coach, and a parent who loves children. He decided to write a children's book series that would appeal to children aged 5-11. He desired to bring powerful lessons and teachings that appealed to children and adults alike while creating an interesting tale. He realized that there is a dearth of excellent material for children containing important life principles while still providing fun, interactive, and magical stories. Furthermore, David K. is the Chief Spiritual Officer for LoveMakers Foundation, a Non-Profit Spiritual Organization based on LOVE.

About the Illustrator

Karen Light is the Founder, Illustrator, and Creativity Coach at Studio Light Illustration. Karen partners with authors to nurture humanity through the magic of story-telling. She believes that stories connect us as humans, forge understanding, evoke empathy, and challenge us to think of ways to create a world in which all living creatures can thrive! Karen can also be found hiking, swing dancing, travelling, spending time with loved ones, or curled up with a good book.

www.ingramcontent.com/pod-product-compliance
Lightning Source LLC
Chambersburg PA
CBHW041706160426

43209CB00017B/1762